SAP MM Certification Questions, Answers, and Explanations

By Jordan Schliem

Please visit our website at www.sapcookbook.com

ISBN 0975305263

Hello,

Thank you for buying this book. I've spent some time designing it so that you might find it a purposeful and efficient way to meet your objectives. The MM Q&A Book was intended for those who want to be able to ask meaningful questions of their prospective hires of course, but it is also a fine tool for the consultant to practice his interviewing skills, or simply learn more about SAP MM.

MM Q&A is split up into three distinct flavors of questions. The first section of the book contains questions that will allow you to ascertain your prospective employee's/contractor's grasp of the "Big Picture". These questions were purposefully created with the intent of drawing out a person's overall understanding of the procurement cycle. The next section of the book is filled with questions dealing with configuration. Proper answers here should give you the assurance that the person you're interviewing knows where to go to properly customize your system to your needs. Lastly, the third section of this book will gives you questions that will prove actual hand-on experience using the system. The day to day activities and troubleshooting skills necessary to properly train, debug, and test for your MM implementation.

Now, although the answers presented here are tested, tried, and true, it may be more enlightening for you to look more for the logical steps involved in an answer. Some of the conceptual questions aside (a Purchase Order is a Purchase Order), there are sometimes many differing ways to achieve the same objective in SAP's MM, but the logic of attacking most problems will be fairly universal. Also, I've found that a person who doesn't know the answer to a problem, but has a good plan of attack (for getting the information), possesses a strong trait. For the ultimate example of this line of thought, check out the last question in this book. It probably is too specific and nobody will believe that you're asking them this with a straight face. Go ahead and throw it at them though...the way the question is handled will lend much more light on a person's competence than what is specifically said. I wish you the best of luck and I hope this book serves you well.

Jordan Schliem

Laguna Niguel, California

Motivation

During the course of an average project, I am usually called upon by a project manager to "help screen resources" for different parts of the project. And one thing comes to mind – if done properly, it's very time consuming, and it's really hard work!

My interviews usually sound something like this –

Jim: "Please rate yourself, on a scale of 1-10 on your SRM knowledge and experience..."

Interviewee: "Um, probably something like 10..."

Jim: "OK, so, let me just say something... I don't believe there is such a thing as a ten."

Interviewee: "What would you rate yourself?"

Jim: "I rate myself an 8."

Interviewee: "Why so low?"

Jim: "There's no such thing as a ten. All of the nines are working at SAP, SAP Labs, or SAP Consulting, and so basically that puts me at about an eight. But we're here to talk about ***your*** skills. And so you think you're a 10, huh? OK, so tell me what you know about debugging the n-step approval workflow..."

And then I try to ask the questions that truly flesh out a person's understanding of the software. It's part science, part art to be sure – but the #1 thing I'm looking for in an interview is that the resource represents their skills truthfully. The good resources know what they know, know what they don't know, and they're open about it.

And so I hope that this book will serve as a much-needed guide for managers trying to get the right resource for their project. If you construct an interview based on these questions, I'm confident you can get a good idea about the depth and breadth of a consultant's experiences and accumulated knowledge.

Jim Stewart

President EquityPress

Detroit, Michigan

August 2005

Introduction

This book is divided into three parts – conceptual questions related to MM, questions dealing with MM configuration, and finally, questions designed to let us have an understanding of an applicant's practical knowledge and troubleshooting skills.

Each interview question has a question and an answer – that is pretty straightforward – but when you see the guru icon – this is information that represents the highest degree of knowledge in a particular area. So if you're looking for a "guru" be sure to listen for an answers similar to those given under the guru icon.

Don't be bamboozled!

The SAP Guru has Spoken!

Part I: Conceptual Questions

Question 1: What MRP procedures are available in MM-CBP (Consumption Based Planning)?

A: Various material planning methods are used in MRP (Material Requirements Planning).

Reorder point procedure (VM)
Forecast-based planning (VV)
Time-Phased materials planning (PD)

These are specified in material creation (MM01) under the MRP 1 tab.

Question 2: Under what conditions are "planned orders" created? What may planned orders be converted to and how is that conversion accomplished?

A: Planned orders are always created when the system creates an internal procurement proposal. In the case of vendor procurement, the MRP Controller may create a planned order or directly create a PR. The next step for a planned order is to be converted to a PR so it goes to purchasing and is to eventually become a PO. A planned order can be converted to a PR using transaction code MD14.

Question 3: What are the organizational levels of the Enterprise Structure in R/3?

A: The top level of the organizational plan is the Client, followed by Company Code, which represents a unit with its own accounting, balance, P&L, and possibly identity (subsidiary). The next level down is Plant, an operational unit within a company (HQ, Assembly Plant, Call Center, etc.). The Purchasing Organization is the legally responsibly group for external transactions. This group is further subdivided into Purchasing Groups.

Question 4: What are the different ways to organize purchasing organizations?

A: A Purchasing Organization may be responsible for multiple plants and this is referred to as "Distributed Purchasing". On the other hand, "Centralized Purchasing" features one Purchasing Organization per Plant.

A Purchasing Organization doesn't necessarily need to be assigned to a Company Code. This would enable procurement for every company code as long as buyers are acting for an individual Plant, and that Plant is assigned to the Purchasing Organization. Hence, a plant may be assigned to more than one Purchasing Organization.

Question 5: What are "Special Stocks"?

A: Special Stocks are stocks that are accounted for but are not owned by the client, or are not stored at a regular facility. Consignment, sales order, and project stock are examples.

Question 6: What are some of the options available to transfer materials from one plant to another?

A: Although it is possible to transfer materials from one plant to another without a Stock Transport Order, many advantages are lost including entering a vendor number, planning a goods receipt in the receiving plant, monitoring process from PO history, and the ability to create STO directly from a MRP PR.

Question 7: What are some of the common Stock Transport Order Movement Types?

A: One step transfers of materials can be posted using MT 301. Other various transport scenarios differ in the MTs by the Goods Issues and Good Receipts. Common Goods Issues may use MTs 303, 351, 641, or 643 in the STO. A STOs Good Receipt often uses MT 101.

Question 8: What is the difference between a Purchase Order and a Purchase Requisition?

A: A Purchase Requisition is a document type that gives notification of a need for materials or services. A Purchase Order is a document type that is a formal request for materials or services from an outside vendor or plant. Procurement types may be defined at the line item and can be standard, subcontracting, consignment, stock transfer, or an external service.

Question 9: What is an "indirectly created" Purchase Requisition?

A: An indirectly created Purchase Requisition has been initiated by CBP, the PS Project System, PM Maintenance, and Service Management, or PP Production Planning and Control. The "directly created" Purchase Requisition, on the other hand, is created by a person manually in the requesting department specifying what materials/services, units, and a delivery date.

Question 10: What is an RFQ and how is it different from the Quotation Form?

A: A RFQ is a purchasing document and an invitation to a vender(s) for quotation regarding needed materials or services. If multiple an RFQ is sent to multiple vendors, the system can automatically determine the best quote and send rejection letters in response to all others. The RFQ and the Quotation Form are one in the same in the system as vendor's quotes are entered directly in the RFQ.

Question 11: What are the transactions that will result in a change of stock?

A: A Goods Receipt is a posting acknowledging the arrival of materials from a vendor or production, which results in an increase in warehouse stock, a Goods Issue which results in a reduction in stock, or a Stock Transfer moving materials from one location to another.

Question 12: When would it be prudent to post goods movements via the Shipping Application?

A: If picking, packing, and transportation operations need to be planned in detail. Also, in shipping, you can manage movements like returns from customers, vendors, and returns to stock. Movement Types in shipping start with a 6.

Question 13: What is a Reservation?

A: A Reservation is a document used to make sure that the warehouse keeps a certain amount of a material or materials ready for transfer at a later date. It contains information on what, quantity, when, where from and to. Reservations help effective procurement by utilizing the MRP system to avoid out of/lack of stock situations.

Question 14: Can you manually generate a Purchase Requisition referencing a Purchase Order or a Scheduling Agreement?

A: A Purchase Requisition cannot be created with reference to either of these, as they are documents controlled by the purchasing organizations.

Requirements can be automatically generated with MRP that reference a Scheduling Agreement if the source list is maintained for item-vendor combination.

Question 15: How is GR/IR account related to Inventory? □

A: If you are involved with inventory, then you need the GR/IR account (Inventory Account) when the IR is posted. If you are not involved about inventory, then the system does not need the GR/IR account when the IR is posted; the system needs a G/L instead of the GR/IR account.

Question 16: How do planned and unplanned consumption affect Movement Types?

A: In a customized Movement Type, you have defined which consumption value gets posted in the movement. Many will always be planned or unplanned, but for some there is a dependency on if the movement references a reservation. This would be planned consumption.

Question 17: What are Departmental Views?

A: All functional areas of the system use the same material master data. The material master data is defined in individual screens (departmental views) that can be added as needed. Thus a material can be created with only basic data and other departments can add other information later as it becomes available.

Question 18: Is Material Data valid for all organizational levels?

A: Control of master data depends largely on how each company sets up its Organizational levels - centralized or decentralized. Some material data is valid for all organizational levels while other data is valid only at certain levels. (I.e.: client, plant, sales org., etc.).

Question 19: Why would you want to create physical inventory sheets to perform an inventory cycle-count on a material or materials?

A: For a cycle counting procedure, physical inventory documents need to be created. These are used to record inventory levels of the material being cycle counted.

Use transaction MICN. Click on the Execute button. On screen "Batch Input: Create Physical Inventory Documents for Cycle Counting", perform the following, Click on the Generate Session button and Click on the Process Session button. This procedure details how to create the physical inventory documents for cycle counting in a batch, rather than one at a time, based on certain criteria. This would print physical inventory documents for all material/batches that meet those requirements.

Question 20: What is the difference between a Blanket Purchase Order and the Framework Order?

A: In general, the Blanket POs are used for consumable materials such as office paper with a short text, with item category B. There need not be a corresponding master record, for the simplicity of the procurement. The FO, Framework Order, document type is used. Here, the PO validity period as well as the limits are to be mentioned.

The GR, or Service Entry for the PO are not necessary in the case of Blanket POs. One need not mention the account assignment category during creation of the PO. It can be U, or unknown and be changed at the time of IR.

Question 21: What is Release Procedure?

A: Release Procedure is approving certain documents like PRs or POs by criteria defined in the configuration. It is sensible to define separate release procedures for different groups of materials for which different departments are responsible, and to define separate procedures for investment goods and consumption goods.

Question 22: If you have a multi-line-item PO, can you release the PO item by item?

A: No, a PO is released at the header level meaning a total release or "With Classification".

PRs, on the other hand, have two release procedures possible. "With Classification" as described above, and "Without Classification" where it is only possible to release the PR item by item.

Question 23: What is a Material Type?

A: A Material Type describes the characteristics of a material that are important in regards to Accounting and Inventory Management. A material is assigned a type when you create the material master record. "Raw Materials", "Finished Products", and "Semi-Finished Products" are examples. In the standard MM module, the Material Type of ROH denotes an externally procured material, and FERT indicates that the relevant material is produced in-house.

Question 24: What is a price comparison?

A: Perform a price comparison using ME49 and one may compare quotations from different vendors.

Question 25: What is a Source List?

A: The Source List identifies preferred sources of supply for certain materials. If it's been maintained, it will ID both the source of supply and the time period. The Source List facilitates gaining a fixed source of supply, blocked source of supply, and/or helps us to select the proffered source during the source determination process.

Question 26: What are the various "steps" in the MM Cycle from material creation through invoice?

A: The following creates a rough picture of the MM Cycle. Create material, create vendor, assign material to vendor, procure raw material through PR, locate vendor for certain material, processing GR, goods issue, and invoice verification.

Question 27: Give some examples of the information relating to a material's storage/warehousing?

A: Some examples are Unit of Issue, Storage Conditions, Packaging Dimensions, Gross Weight, Volume, and Hazardous Materials Number. Also, there are various Storage Strategies information and options.

Question 28: What are the various features of Consignment Stocks?

A: Consignment Stocks remain the legal property of the Vendor until the organization withdraws the material from the consignment stores. The invoice can be due at set periods of time, for example monthly, and it is also a configuration possibility that the organization will take ownership of the stock after a certain period of time. Consignment Stock is allocated to the available stock because the Consignment Stock is managed under the same material number as your company's stock.

The most important characteristic of Consignment Stock is that it isn't valuated. When the material is withdrawn, it is valuated at the price of the respective vendor. Before procuring the stock, consideration should be given if one consignment is coming from multiple vendors. If so, we can manage all of them independently at the price of the individual vendors. In the Info Record, we will maintain three different prices for the same material for three different vendors.

Question 29: What is a Quotation?

A: Once a vendor has received an RFQ, the vendor will send back a quote that will be legally binding for a certain period of time. Specifically, a Quotation is an offer by a vendor to a purchasing organization regarding the supply of material(s) or performance of service(s) subject to specified conditions. The Quotation then need to be maintained in the "Maintain Quotation: XXXX" screens.

Question 30: What is the Source List?

A: The Source List identifies preferred sources of supply for certain materials. If the Source List has been properly maintained, it will identify both the source of a material and the period of time in which you can order the material from the source.

Question 31: What is an Invoice Verification?

A: The Invoice Verification component completes the material procurement process and allows credit memos to be processed. Invoice Verification includes entering invoices and credit memos that have been received, checking accuracy of invoices with respect to price and arithmetic, and checking block invoices (these are the ones which differ too much from the original PO).

Question 32: What are the different types of Invoice Verification?

A: Invoices based on Purchase Orders. With purchase-order-based Invoice Verification, all of the items of a purchase order can be settled together, regardless of whether or not an item has been received in several partial deliveries. All of the deliveries are totaled and posted as one item.
Invoices based on Goods Receipts. With goods-receipt-based Invoice Verification, each individual goods receipt is invoiced separately.
Invoices without an order reference. When there is no reference to a PO, it is possible to post the transaction directly to a Material Account, a G/L Account, or an Asset Account.

You can park Invoices that reference POs and GRs as well as Invoices with no reference in the system. When you park a document or change a parked document, neither substitution nor validation is supported. The system only carries out these functions after you actually post a parked document.

Question 33: Why would an organization need to allow Negative Stocks?

A: Negative Stocks are necessary when Goods Issues are entered necessarily (business process reasons) prior to the corresponding Goods Receipts and the material is already located physically in the warehouse.

Part II: Configuration Related Questions

Question 34: How do you create a movement type? When will movement type numbers be odd?

A: When prompted by a dialog box after an activity, you copy a movement type. Select the field "Movement Type" and "Continue". In the Define Work area, enter the movement type to be copied in *From:* and the name your new movement type in the *To:* field. Now choose *Continue*. Choose the desired movement type you want then choose *Edit → Copy as* and re-type the selected movement type with the new type copy all dependent entries and make sure to begin with a proper prefix (9,X,Z). All control indicators are copied to the new movement type. Review the new movement type changing any necessary controls. Reversal movement types are numbered as the number type plus one. The reversal for movement type 451 (Returns From Customer) is 452. As a last step before saving your settings, add a copy the reversal movement type and enter it in *Reversal/follow-on movement types.*

Question 35: How do you adopt standard settings for the Message Determination Facility In MM-PUR?

A: The Message Determination Facility is by default active and message determination schema is supplied for all purchasing documents including POs, PRs, RFQs etc.

All of the desired message types must be maintained. Choose Master data → Messages → Purchasing document → Create or Change from the Purchasing menu. Add the message type and pick the key combination. The key combination decides the condition table where the condition record is stored. Enter all needed items. Next screen, create the individual condition records. Using the menu options Goto → Means of Communication, enter the proper peripheral, or output for each message record. Save.

Question 36: How do you set price control for receipts (goods/invoice) telling the system how to value stocks?

A: Transaction Code OMW1 allows you to set price control to S (Standard Price) or V (Moving Average Price).

Under Standard Price (S), the materials and accounting documents are both valid. The one with the lower value will be posted with a price variance entry.

Question 37: How do you access the Materials Management Configuration Menu?

A: Transaction Code OLMS has a host of options that are not accessible through the IMG.

Question 38: How are the various MM configuration Transactions accessed?

A: Transaction Codes OLMD accesses MM-CBP, OLMB accesses MM-IM, OLME accesses MM-PUR, OLML accesses MM-Warehouse Management, OLMS accesses Material Master Data, and OLMW is the proper transaction for valuation and account assignment.

Question 39: What are some of the more important Materials Management Tables?

A: EINA contains general data of the (Purchasing) Information Record; EINE includes Purchasing Organization of the same. MAKT is the Materials Description table, MARA-General Materials data, MARC-Plant Data for Materials, MARD-Storage Location Data for Material, MAST-Material to BOM Link, MBEW-Material Valuation, and MKPF-Header Material Document.

Some of the tables that directly pertain to the document types are T156 Movement Type and T023/T024 Groups Material and Purchasing.

Question 40: Can you add custom fields to POs and RFQs?

A: Yes. You must add custom fields to the customer including structures I_EKKODB and I_EKPODB.

Create a project via CMOD for enhancement MM06E005. Follow the documentation for MM06E005, and create the sub-screens for function group XM06 using transaction SE80. Add fields to the appropriate screen. It is recommended that you call the screen fields EKPO_CI-name or EKKO_CI-name. This simplifies transferring data to/from the screen. Put code in EXIT_SAPMM06E_018 to transfer data from sub-screen to structure E_CI_EKPO. Put code in EXIT_SAPMM06E_016 to transfer data from database to sub-screen using structure I_CI_EKPO. In the PBO of the sub-screen, do any processing to make fields display only, or hide them. If you need values from the main screen to make decisions in the sub-screen, define variables in the global data part of the function module, and fill the variables in EXIT_SAPMM06E_016 (PBO of main screen) Make sure everything has been activated like user exists, screens, etc.

Question 41: Where can you dictate how Planned Orders are converted into Requisitions in MRP?

A: Look at the Transaction Code OPPR indicator. Assign proper indicator.

Question 42: What SAP program is used to update or create Material Master Records?

A: RMDATIND is used to update Material Master Records and can be used for such assignments as extending all materials to a new plant.

Question 43: What Views are possible for a material?

A: The material type selected controls the views possible for material.

For a material to be used in the system it needs to be created for each plant. Multiple views of a material are possible but at a minimum, the material needs to have a description and a base unit of measure assigned on the basic data view. Additional department views (i.e. Accounting, Sales, Purchasing, MRP, Warehouse) can be added at a later time by extending the material. As additional plants are added, a material will need to be extended to the plants before it can be used there.

Question 44: When can a Production Resource/Tool be defined as a material?

A: A Production Resource / Tool can be defined as a material if purchasing and inventory functions are to be carried out for that PRT.

The information required to be input is dependent upon which department views are being created. Thus, material master information is typically entered at different times by numerous system users. Note that to add a view, the "Create Material" transaction is used rather than the "Change Material" transaction.

Question 45: When creating a new Material, what may prompt some of the possible Material Types?

A: Pressing F4 gives a list of choices. Select the material type for the material you are creating. For example, FHMI for Prod. Resources/tools, ROH for Raw Materials, FERT for Finished Products, etc.

Question 46: How do you determine which views of a material need to be added or to see which plants a material has been extended to?

A: You can use transaction MM50.

To extend a material to a different plant requires selecting the new plant on the organizational level screen. Note that all views of a material are not extended unless they were selected on the initial screen. In addition, each plant may have a different system configuration requiring additional inputs on each of the departmental screens. Material changes made in one plant do not change that material in other plants.

Question 47: How can you set user defaults for views and organizational levels?

A: The user defaults for views can be set under Menus: Defaults → Views. Select those views to be checked on by default when generating a new material. Select 'View selection only on request' when the select view pop-up is to be by-passed unless selected.

For organizational levels, Menus: Defaults → organizational levels. Enter those organizational levels to be defaulted when generating a new material. Select 'Org. levels/profiles only on request' when the select view pop-up is to be by-passed unless selected.

Question 48: What needs to be present in order for Material Type to be automatically copied from one view to another?

A: When creating any view, the Industry Sector and Material type will be automatically copied from an existing view, so long as at least one view exists.

Question 49: How do you create a document/e-mail notifying your supplier or internal personnel when an invoice plan is settled?

A: The IMG setting is Material Management → Logistics Invoice Verification → Message Determination.

If these settings are not made, the message "Invoicing Plan: No Message Was Found for Partner XXX, Company Code XXX". If the notifying documents are not required, simply turn off the message by changing the message from "error" to "information" using Material Management → Logistic Invoice Verification → Define Attributes of System Messages.

Question 50: How can one keep users from using standard MM Movement Types?

A: Standard Movement Types should not be deleted from the system. The account assignments, however, may be deleted for a particular Movement Type in table T030 using transaction OBYC.

Another way to achieve the same result is to enter Movement Type in transaction OMJJ. Remove MBXX from allowed transactions.

Question 51: How do you define a Release Procedure for PRs and POs?

A: Use Transaction ME54 and ME28 respectively.

Question 52: How do you Change Characteristic?

A: Use Transaction Code CT04. Follow these steps: Format (numeric, character, etc.), Unit of Measure, Templates, Required Entry, Intervals as Values (?), descriptions for texts for characteristics and characteristic values, display options for characteristics on the value assignment screen, Allowed Values, Default Values that are set automatically on the Value Assignment Screen.

Question 53: How do you create a Class?

A: Class is defined as the group of characteristics, which can be attributed to a product. Use Transaction CL01. Enter the value for the Class name and a small description. Select the group from it. The values on the different tabs are not mandatory, so you can skip the values if you wish or you can go to any extent needed. Save, and the Class is created.

Question 54: How do you configure the Release Procedure?

A: Use Transaction OMGQ.

Question 55: Will ROH have a sales view? Will FERT have a purchasing view?

A: They shouldn't because ROH type materials are procured from the outside not sold and FERT type materials are created inside and aren't procured.

In some special cases, we have to sell raw materials (ROH) and buy finished goods (FERT) from outside sources. The views must be extended in these cases using transactions OMS2 and MM50.

Question 56: Where do we create Vendor Account Groups, or screen layout in Vendor Master?

A: Using SPRO, Financial Accounting → Accounts Payable/Receivable → Vendor Accounts → Master Records → Preparations for Creating Vendor Master Records → Define Account Groups With Screen Layout (Vendors) or
Define Screen Layout Per Activity.

Question 57: What are the key fields for the Material Master?

A: Material Groups, External Material Groups, Divisions, Material Status, Labs & Offices, Basic Materials, Storage Conditions, Temperature Conditions, Container Requirements, and Units or Measure Groups.

Question 58: What are the main Purchasing Tables?

A:

EKBN	Purchase Requisition
EBKN	Purchase Requisition Account Assignment
EKAB	Release Documentation
EKBE	History of Purchase Document

Question 59: How do you create a material?

A: Use Transaction Code MM01. Name the material, choose an industry sector, choose a material type, create or copy the views, add a basic description, give it's attributes/values, MRP information, reorder point, accounting valuation, warehouse management information and then save the data.

Question 60: What are some of the data points provided by Purchasing for a material?

A: Some of the key inputs when creating a material are Base Unit of Measure, Purchasing Group, Reminder days, tolerance levels, shipping instructions, GR processing time, JIT schedule indicator, Critical part (?), etc.

Question 61: What are the Lot Size attributes a material can posses?

A: Lot Sizing dictates the reorder quantity for a material. A material can have a static, periodic, optimum, or fixed lot size.

Question 62: How do you create a Vendor?

A: Use Transaction Code XK01. Add the Vendor name, Company Code, Purchasing Organization, Account Group, and the Vendor address. Next add the country, Bank Key, Bank Account, Account Holder (an actual name), and then save the data.

Question 63: How are materials assigned to vendors?

A: Information Record links materials to the vendor, thus facilitating the process of selecting quotations. Use Transaction Code ME11 or Logistics → Material Management → Purchasing and then Master Data → Info Record → Create.

Question 64: What data does the Information Record contain?

A: The Information Records has data on Units of Measure, Vendor price changes after a certain level, what materials have been procured by a specific vendor, price and conditions for relevant Purchase Organization, Tolerance limits for over/under delivery, Vendor evaluation data, planned delivery time, and availability time the vendor can supply the material.

Question 65: How do you create the Information Record based on the Material Master record?

A: In the IMG, Master Data → Info Record → Create. Enter Vendor Number, Material Number, Purchasing Organization or Plant Number. Enter the number of the Information Record if external number assignments are used (left blank, the system will assign a number). Enter the General Data for the Vendor, order unit, origin data, and supply option, Customs Tariff Number. Next, enter the Vendor's planned delivery time (used for scheduling), responsible Purchasing Group, and Standard PO quantity (used in conjunction with price scales for price determination). Check the Control Data. The tolerance data and the responsible purchasing group are taken as default values from the Material Master record. Enter the net price. Now, from the top of the screen Go To → Texts to display the text overview. You can enter the info memo or the PO text. If the PO text is already defined in the Material Master record, it appears as a default value. Save the record.

Question 66: What are some of the initial configuration steps for Purchase Requisitions?

A: Define Document Types, Processing Time, Release Procedure (with and without classification), Setup Authorization Check for G/L Accounts, Define Number Range.

Question 67: When, in initial configuration, why would you have to Setup Stock Transport Order?

A: If it is required to carry out an inter-plant Stock Transfer through SD, then this configuration is required and must be carried out.

Question 68: What are some of the initial configuration steps for Inventory Management?

A: Plant Parameters, Define System Message Attributes, Number Assignment (Allocate document type FI to transactions), Goods Issues, Transfer Postings, Define Screen Layout, Maintain Copy Rules for Reference Documents, Setup Dynamic Availability Check, Allow Negative Stocks (?).

Question 69: What are some of the initial configuration steps for Physical Inventory?

A: Define Default Values for Physical Inventory Document, Batch Input Reports, Tolerances for Physical Inventory Differences, and Inventory Sampling. Cycle Counting should be configured as well.

Part III: Practical/Troubleshooting Related Questions

Question 70: How can you process vendor returns without a Purchase Order reference?

A: Use Transaction Code ME21N.

Look for the Return columns and click it at the item details,
MIGO_GR , Goods Receipt for Return Purchase Order□ Movement type will be 161 to deduct the stock and 162 for reversal.□ Before saving, check if there is a check in the Return Column to ensure that it is a return Purchase Order.

Question 71: How can an invoice be verified?

A: Transaction Code OLMR may be utilized.

Question 72: How do you change the standard price in the Material Master?

A: The standard price in the Material Master can't be updated in a direct manner. A great way to update it is to fill the fields Future Price MBEW-ZKPRS and the Effective Date MBEW-ZKDAT for the material on the accounting view. Next, go to Logistics → Materials Management → Valuation → Valuation Price Determination → Future Price → Activate. TCODE MR2B, program RMMR2100. Lastly, run the BDC that was created to update the standard price.

Question 73: How do you perform a Goods Receipt?

A: Use Transaction MIGO. Enter the Header Data, select the Movement Type, Enter the PO Number, select the PO items to be copied, and then post the document.

Question 74: How can you post a Goods Receipt if the PO number is not known?

A: If you selected *PO Number Not Known* in Transaction MIGO, you can specify search criteria for the POs on the initial screen. The system then displays a list of purchase orders. Select and copy the required PO items.

Question 75: How do you display a list of all reservations in the system?

A: Run report *RM07RESL.*

Question 76: If you have created a custom Movement Type and you get a "not allowed" error, where should you first look for the cause?

A: Using Transaction Code OMJJ, check "Allowed Transactions" for the customized Movement Types.

Question 77: How do you find the logical value for stock item by date?

A: Use Transaction MC49.

Question 78: How can you disable a Reservation in MRP?

A: Use Transaction Code OPPI to check "block stock".

Question 79: How do you add an attachment to a Purchase Order?

A: One may attach any document to a PO manually without using the Document Management System in SAP, but no attachments can be added while you create a PO using ME21N.
Save your PO and then open the PO using ME22N. There you can attach a document with the Service for Object button. Click the Service Object button → Create → Create Attachment then select your window directory, the file to be attached. This attachment is only for internal information. The system will not print this document automatically along with a PO printout.

Question 80: How do you generate an automatic PO after creating a PR using a particular material?

A: In MMR and VMR check Auto PO (MM02/XK02).

Maintain the Source List and select the indicator for the source list record as MRP relevant (ME01). If more than one source list record is generated, make one of them fixed. Run MRP and the PRs generated will be pre-assigned with the source of supply (MD01). Enter ME59 for automatically creating POs from PRs.

Question 81: Where is the Header level and Item level data saved in a PO?

A: In SE11, we can see this information in table EKKO and EKP0 respectively.

Question 82: Where is Material Master data saved?

A: Tables MARA and MARC.

Question 83: How do we know if a PO has been issued?

A: Bring the Requisition up by using Material Management → Purchasing → Purchase Requisition → Display. Where the requisition overview screen is displayed, select an item by clicking on the selection box to the left of the item. Click on the General Statistics icon on the application tool bar. Select item. General Statistics icon. The screen appears, in the middle, under Order Statistics, in the field Purchase Order, if there is no number the PO has not been issued.

Question 84: What is the difference between a PR with a Master Record and without a Master Record for the material being ordered?

A: If the master record exists, then all of the information about the Source List, Information Record, and Vendor Evaluation already exist in the system. If we don't have a Master record for the material we are ordering, the material is generally being ordered for direct usage or consumption. You can specify which consumption account is to be charged which is also known as Account Assignment. For example, we assign the purchase costs associated with a requisition to our sales order or cost center.

If the first situation exists, many times purchasing enters into a longer-term purchasing agreement with a Vendor, which is called an "Outline Agreement". If the Outline Agreement is done, then Purchasing cannot issue a purchase order against a PR. It can only set up such an agreement (either a "Contract" or a "Scheduling Agreement").

Question 85: Can you change a Purchase Requisition after it has been created?

A: Yes. Use Transaction ME52N. Check to see if the PR has already had a PO issued against it. If so, you must inform the Purchasing Group. Check if the PR has been approved. If so, you may only make changes to a limited extent and may be subject of approval. Check if the PR was created by MRP. In this case, you don't have much control over the modification process.

All changes to items are logged and stored. Information stored includes when the information was changed, who changed it, what the changes were, etc. Select the desired item in the item overview and choose Go To → Statistics → Changes.

Question 86: How do we create Consignment Stocks?

A: Everything is the same as a normal PR or PO, except: Enter the item category "K" for the consignment item. This ensures that the Goods Receipt is posted to the consignment stores and an invoice receipt cannot be generated for the item. Also, do not enter a net price.

Question 87: What is Vendor Evaluation and how do you maintain it?

A: Vendor Evaluation helps you select the Source of Supply by a score assigned to a particular vendor. The scores are on a scale of 1 to 100 and are based on differing criteria. Use Transaction ME61 and enter the Purchasing Organization and Vendor Number.

Question 88: What are the components of the Master Data that details a company's procurement; used by, Vendor Evaluation for example?

A: The key components of Master Data are: Info Record (ME11), Source List (ME01), Quota Arrangement (MEQ1), Vendor (MK01), Vendor Evaluation (ME61), and Condition Type (MEKA).

Question 89: How do we get a proper list of vendors to send an RFQ?

A: Either use the Information Record to see who has sold a particular material to the organization in the past, or go through the Source List.

Question 90: How do you create a Source List?

A: Use Transaction ME01. Enter the Material Number and the Plant Data. Enter source list records, validity period, period of time material is procurable, Vendor Number, responsible Purchasing Organization (or number of the Agreement or Contract), PPL (if the material can be procured from another plant), Fixed Source (?), MRP control.

Also, a check should be done to see whether any source list records overlap. To do so, choose Source List → Check.

Question 91: How will items be returned to the vendor?

A: When you are posting a Goods Receipt for a PO, you can also enter items that you want to return to the vendor. To do this, you no longer have to reference the purchase order with which the goods were originally delivered. From the item overview, choose 161 (Return for PO) as the default value for the Movement Type. Enter the data for the return item(s) and post the document.

Question 92: Where do you perform a Goods Issue?

A: Use Transaction MIGO.

It is possible that when MIGO is accessed that a different document screen appears than the one required. This occurs because SAP remembers the last Goods Movement transaction accessed per user login. To reach the Goods Issue Purchase Order screen, click the Dropdown Icon in the transaction field and select "Goods Issue".

Question 93: How do you perform a Goods Issue?

A: Use Transaction MIGO. On the initial screen, enter the header data (you need not enter the Movement Type or the Plant as these are automatically copied from the order). Choose Goods Issue → Create with Reference → To Order… If you know the order number, enter it directly. Using the By-products Indicator, you can simultaneously post the Goods Receipt of planned by-products. Using the Choose transaction/events indicator, you can display all transactions/events for an order and choose the transaction/events for which you want to post a Goods Issue. Copy the desired item(s). Check data on the overview screen. Post the document.

Question 94: How do you perform an Invoice Verification?

A: If the Invoice refers to an existing document (PO, etc.), then the system pulls up all of the relevant information like Vendor, Material, Quantity, Terms of Delivery, and Payment Terms etc. When the Invoice is entered, the system will find the relevant account. Automatic posting for Sales Tax, Cash Discount, Corrections etc. When the Invoice is posted, certain data such as Average Price of Material and Price History are updated. Use Transaction MIRO.

Question 95: How do you display parked documents?

A: There are two possible transactions to use here. They are FB03 and FBV3. The first shows all posted document types. This is the best choice if you think the document has been posted to you actual balance. The later shows only parked documents that have not yet posted to your expenditure balance. These documents are still encumbrances. It is the best choice if you are trying to find which documents are still awaiting completion or approval.

This transaction is very similar to the FBV2 transaction used with P-Card reconciliation and marking parked documents complete.

Question 96: **What do the W, V, and F fields show about the status of a document in FBV3?**

A: An X under the W column means the document is subject to Workflow. Most documents on this screen should have an X in this column. However, not all documents are subject to workflow (cash deposits etc.). An X in the V column means that the document has been marked as complete. If they are subject to Workflow, they have been sent to Workflow for approval when they were marked complete. An X in the F column means that the document has been approved and posted to expenditures. This column will always be empty in this screen.

An X under W, but no X under V means that you have not marked the document as complete. If it hasn't been marked as complete, use FBV2 to check the document and, if it is correct, mark it as complete. You can quickly go to the document from the list screen by double clicking on the document number. When the document is displayed, click on Document on the menu bar, and then click on Change in the drop down menu. The transaction will switch from FBV3-Display to FBV2-Change. An X under both W and V will mean it is waiting for approval and you may need to check the approval path to see if has met with a delay.

Question 97: If you are using Transaction MRKO, vendor settlement, and we get an error message (FS217 or M8443 etc.), how would you go about troubleshooting this?

A: I'd have to be a Guru to answer this!

(With this question, look for an answer that follows a similar logic)

To troubleshoot this problem, we have these steps to follow. Set up Output Condition Type "KONS". The Output Type specifies the kind of output to be produced. The Output Type is predefined for your area of the R/3 system. If alternative choices are possible, you can, of course, list them by pressing F4. The Output Type can specify, for example, a printed form that you need for internal use or a form that you want to send to a customer or vendor (for example, an order confirmation). The Output Type can also be an internal electronic mail message that you want to send to staff in another department. To create an Output Type, we use Transaction V/30. Click on New Entries; go to where you can define a new Output Type (i.e. KONS). Once you have fed all of the data in the screen you can save it and we will have a new Output Type. Now, use Transaction MRM1 where we will maintain conditions for the Output Type KONS. When you press the Key combination tab, you go to the "Create Condition Records (Consignment): Fast Entry" screen. Here you define the Company Code, partner etc. Hit the save button. Now you have conditions associated with the Output Type KONS. Now, we must maintain the appropriate Tax Code in the Information Record. Use Transaction ME12. Be sure Info Category is consignment. Hit <Enter> and you will go to the screen "Purch. Org. data 1". Hit <Enter> again and you will go to the next screen where you need to maintain the Tax Codes. Put in Tax Code "I0" which means exempt. The next step would be to go to the G/L Account and update the "Tax Category" using Transaction FS00. "Drop down" the box for Tax Category and you will get some options. Choose the first option "-" Only Input Tax Allowed. Hit Save. The next step, go to check the "Field Status Compatibility at G/L Account"; use Transaction SE38. Now, enter the program number "RM07CUFA" and hit "Execute". Now enter Movement Type "291 K" which is used for the Goods Issue related to consignment. When you press the Execute button, you will see screen "Field Selection Comparison: Movement Type – G/L Account". Now, check the Compatibilities of all the fields, if a particular is not compatible, then there will be an Error message with a Red Highlight.

Now the signs Plus, Minus, and dot denote whether the entry in that particular field is "Required", "Optional", or "Suppressed" etc. Now, the error could be because of the following reasons: If the Mvt column has a "+" and Account column has a "-"; If the Mvt column has a "-" and the Account column has a "+". Once you fix the value you can go to the Error Log and see if there are any more errors there. The last step would be to run Transaction MRKO. Now, you get all of the "Not Settled", "Pending Transactions", or Good Receipts recently done. Then, go to the previous screen and press the "Settle" tab and execute it again for settling the documents. Now the transaction goes through and the vendors are paid automatically. If after doing this, we still get the error message, then we could also go to Transaction OMRM and change the error message to a warning message. The other place to find the error messages is Transaction SE31.

INDEX

M

N

O

P

Q

R

S

T

V

W

ABOUT THE AUTHOR

Jordan Schliem resides in Laguna Niguel, California. He has over ten years of IT experience, most recently in the area of SAP Materials Management and Supplier Relationship Management. He has acted as senior consultant to many Fortune 500 organizations, and has conducted global blueprinting exercises, completed configuration from scratch, perfomed end-user training, and has also been involved in some of the most technically involved enhancements. Mr. Schliem is a graduate of the University of California at Riverside.

www.ingramcontent.com/pod-product-compliance
Lightning Source LLC
LaVergne TN
LVHW091102150826
845673LV00002B/687

9780975305263